It Couldn't Happen to Me:

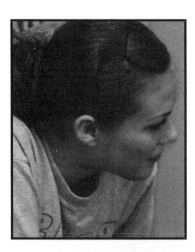

Three
True
Stories
of
Teenage
Moms

Beth Johnson

 THE TOWNSEND LIBRARY

It Couldn't Happen to Me:
Three True Stories of Teenage Moms

TP THE TOWNSEND LIBRARY

For more titles in the Townsend Library,
visit our website: **www.townsendpress.com**

Photography: Beth Johnson

Copyright © 2005 by Townsend Press.
Printed in the United States of America

0 9 8 7 6 5 4 3 2 1

Townsend Press, Inc.
1038 Industrial Drive
West Berlin, New Jersey 08091

ISBN 1-59194-049-4

Library of Congress Control Number:
2005923000

Contents

"I didn't think it could happen to me."

Of the more than 800,000 American teenagers who get pregnant every year, few are prepared to hear the words, "You're going to have a baby." Even fewer are the young girls who are realistically prepared for what it means to bear and raise a child.

"I thought I was too young to get pregnant."

"I thought you couldn't get pregnant the first time."

"He said I didn't have to worry."

The explanations all amount to the same thing: "I didn't think it could happen to *me*."

The fact is, it can and does happen, over and over again, to unmarried teenagers. You, reading these words: If you are a sexually active girl, *it can happen to you.*

The three young women profiled in this book–Johanna, Rasheedah, and Rachel—didn't think it would happen to them, either.

"I didn't worry about getting pregnant," said Johanna, 22, mother of 4-year-old Kiara. "When you're as young and dumb as we were, you just do what you're going to do without thinking about the consequences. You think you know it all, and that nothing bad can happen to you."

Rachel, who became pregnant at 14, thought she was too young to become a mother. Her daughter Payten is now 4.

And 20-year-old Rasheedah, whose little girl Iyonna is 5, says, "I didn't let myself think about pregnancy."

Johanna, Rasheedah, and Rachel have agreed to share their stories in this book, in hopes that other young women can learn something from them. All three have gone through lonely, scary, depressing, and painful times. They have traded their teenage freedom for responsibilities that make them sometimes seem far older than their years. All are raising their daughters alone; none is still involved with her baby's father.

In some ways, all of them have exceeded the expectations society has of teen mothers. All three have earned their high school degrees or GEDs. Two are in college. All are devoted parents, doing their best to raise their daughters well.

Still, the odds continue to be against them. And those odds affect not only them, but their children and their communities. The statistics concerning teenage parenthood are grim. Here are a few to consider:

For the mothers

- Teen moms rarely complete their educations. Less than one-third of girls who have a baby before age 18 ever earn a high school degree. Only 1.5% earn a college degree by age 30.

- The majority of teen mothers never move beyond low-paying, entry-level jobs. Most live in poverty. About 80% of teenage mothers eventually go on welfare.

● Teen moms are at high risk for pregnancy-related health problems. They are more likely than older mothers to develop high blood pressure and anemia, to miscarry or go into premature labor, and to contract sexually transmitted diseases.

● Many teen moms do not receive adequate pre-natal (meaning "before delivery") medical care. During the important first three months of pregnancy, many young girls are still in denial about their pregnancy and do not see a doctor. They are less likely to eat a good diet and take prenatal vitamins, and more likely to smoke, drink, and use drugs than older mothers.

For the children

● The babies of teen moms are at risk for pre-mature birth and low birth weight. Both those conditions increase the chance that the baby will die or develop blindness, deafness, long-term respiratory problems, mental retardation, and other disabilities. Low birth weight doubles the chance that the child will later develop dyslexia or hyperactivity.

- Children of teen moms often do not receive adequate parenting. Even if they try their best, teen moms (and dads, if they are involved) are typically not ready to provide the kind of stable environment, mental stimulation, and the firm but loving discipline that children need.

- Children of teen moms are at risk for abuse. Reports of abuse or neglect occur twice as often in families headed by a teenage mother than in other families. Children of teen moms are about twice as likely to end up in foster care.

- Children of teen moms rarely excel in school. They are far more likely to repeat grades; they score lower on standardized tests; and they are much less likely to graduate from high school than other children.

- Boys born to teen mothers are 13% more likely to end up in prison that other boys. Girls born to teen mothers are 22% more likely to become teen moms themselves.

For the community

- Because teen moms often drop out of school and cannot get good jobs, and because their children often require extra social services (public assistance, foster care, subsidized health care, etc.) there is a huge financial cost to the whole society. In the United States, the annual costs related to teen pregnancy are estimated to be about $7 billion.

- And the cost to society is not only financial. Teenage pregnancies are associated with a number of social problems. Teen parenthood is often part of a cycle—a cycle that can include poverty, lower educational levels, alcohol and substance abuse, crime, and homelessness. These are problems that affect everyone.

Statistics like these are useful. They help to make the case that when girls have babies at a young age, the consequences are often bad for the girl, the baby, and everyone else. What these statistics don't do is address this question:

When it seems clear that an unmarried teenage girl is not the best possible parent, why do so many girls continue getting pregnant?

Surprisingly, out of all developed nations, the United States has the highest rate of out-of-wedlock pregnancy. This is true even though condoms and spermicidal foams are available at most drug stores. A family doctor or clinic can prescribe more reliable contraceptives, including birth-control pills, injections (such as Depo-Provera), or contraceptive implants (such as Norplant). Abstinence (choosing not to be sexually active) is a 100 percent guarantee against pregnancy. With all these options available, why do so many young girls become pregnant?

The answers are many, of course. One that is frequently overlooked is that some young girls want to become pregnant, at least on some level. For the most part, these are girls who don't foresee a bright future for themselves. Susan L. Davies is a researcher who has studied teen pregnancy. "Young girls who are headed to college aren't thinking about getting pregnant," she says. "But if you are a sophomore in a lousy high school and getting terrible grades, and the best that you can hope for is a job at the Dairy Queen, then dropping out and having a baby may seem like your best option." The sad irony is that becoming a teen mom pretty well guarantees a dead-end future for such a girl—and her child.

In many other cases, a girl is trying to deny the fact that she is sexually active—even to herself.

"I think it's the same behavior you sometimes see in someone who has health problems—heart disease or diabetes, for example," says Jhoselyn Martinez.

Jhoselyn, who was a young unmarried mom, is now a college graduate and a radio producer in Philadelphia. "Once you go to the doctor and ask for help, you're acknowledging what is happening. When you say those words,

Jhoselyn Martinez

'I need contraceptives,' you're admitting to yourself what you're doing. Then you have to start thinking of the possible consequences. That's very scary. A lot of people prefer denial.

"For me, raised as a Catholic, it was a big sin to have sex outside of marriage," continues Jhoselyn. "I was afraid I was disappointing God, as well as disappointing my parents. I felt so guilty, and talking frankly to a doctor would have just compounded my guilt. For me, and I think for a lot of girls, it's just easier to pretend that it's not happening. That way you can keep it at a mental distance."

The problem, of course, is that "keeping it at a distance" only works until pregnancy occurs. Then the harsh realities of teen pregnancy become all too real.

One person who has experienced those realities from several angles is Julia Burney of Racine, Wisconsin. Now in her 50s, Julia was born in Mississippi to a 13-year-old mother and her 17-year-old husband. (In those days, among poor people in the rural South, such early marriages were not as unusual as they are today.) Julia herself became an unmarried teen mother, having three children before she turned 20. Later she became a police officer and then founder of Racine's Cops 'n Kids Reading Center. In both those roles, she has spent a great deal

Julia Burney

of time with teenage moms. She works with their children at the Reading Center, and she often speaks to groups of teen moms, encouraging them to be the best parents they can be.

Julia's own children have turned out well. All are educated professional people. But she bluntly discourages anyone else from following her example.

"I never should have had children at such a young age," she says emphatically. "Getting pregnant as a teen—it's the worst thing in the world for a girl and her baby. It really is. Being a good mother when you're 30 is hard. It's nearly impossible when you're a teen.

"You're not grown up yourself when you're a teen mom," Julia explains. "I was, in some ways, about as prepared as a person could be. I was the oldest of ten children, and I'd been helping to raise all those younger ones. But that's not the same as being a mother yourself."

According to Julia, teen moms are constantly

faced with a choice they are not prepared to make. "You're hearing, 'Stay home and be a mother to that baby.' But you're thinking, 'I'm a kid! I'm only 16.' Staying home doesn't feel like the logical choice. What feels right and natural is to act 16—to go with your friends to the mall, to go out partying. It's hard to sit home with a crying baby and look out the window and see your friends running around. A lot of teen moms—not all of them, but most of them— choose that 16-year-old lifestyle. And it's the babies who pay the price."

Julia believes teens often decide to have babies without considering what being a parent truly means. "You know what a lot of teen parents make me think of?" she asks. "That movie, *101 Dalmatians.* When it first came out, everyone had to get a Dalmatian puppy because they looked so cute in the film. And six months later, the pounds were full of Dalmatians because people weren't prepared to take care of them."

Like those dog owners, she says, teens too often

have a baby, then realize they don't want the responsibility. "Even a puppy deserves a responsible owner," says Julia. "So think how much more important and precious a baby is. A baby isn't a novelty. It's not a means to hold a man. Lord knows that doesn't work. That guy who says, 'I love you—I want you to have my shorty'—he's not going to stick around. And when the guy is gone, the baby becomes a pawn, an unwanted pawn. And none of it is that baby's fault."

For girls who already have babies, Julia's advice is direct. "If you don't know how to be a parent, learn how. Go take some classes. Get advice from some grandparents. Find some mentors in mothering. Get involved in your child's school. Do those 'real mom' things, like joining the PTA and packing your child's lunch."

And every minute, Julia says, a teen parent should keep this thought in mind: "It is not that child's fault that his mother is 14, 15, 16. That's a situation the baby never asked for, and it's up to you to try to make that up to him."

How can a teen mom do that? According to Julia, a girl with a baby needs to face this hard fact: she's given up the option to live an ordinary teen life, period. "Make that child your priority," she says. "Get routines in your life, and in the child's. Read your baby bedtime stories; give baths at a regular time; have a regular bedtime for your child; get your son or daughter up in the morning and make them breakfast and make sure they're ready for school—all that real mom stuff. Doing those things isn't easy, but it's right. And it's rewarding to see your child grow up right."

And if a girl is not yet pregnant, Jhoselyn Martinez has some advice for her: "Think more about yourself and your own worth. Is becoming sexually involved with someone a way to gain affection? Is it the result of pressure from your partner? Is it something that is ultimately going to be a positive force in your life? Because as you make those life-altering decisions, the bottom line always ought to be your respect for yourself and your body and your future."

"You're going to have a baby." To a woman who is ready to hear those words, they can be the source of enormous joy. To a girl who is not—and to her child—they can bring about years of sadness, disappointment, and lost opportunities. This book, including Johanna's, Rachel's, and Rasheedah's stories, is presented in the hopes that someday, every child will be wanted, welcomed, and well-prepared for.

Rachel

Rachel Griffith

"**W**here's the green block?" asks the teenager.

"THERE it is!" crows the little girl, waving it triumphantly in the air.

"That's right! Can you show me the pink one?"

"Pink, pink, pink, pink," the 3-year-old sings to herself, touching one block after another. She picks up the green one again and offers it to the girl.

"No, that's green," the older girl says gently. "Can you find a pink one? Pink like your shirt?"

The little girl glances at her shirt, then at the line of blocks lying on the carpet. She snatches up the pink one this time. "I got it!" she announces happily.

"Yay! Good girl!" the teen says, applauding. The little girl beams and begins clapping too.

"Payten is so smart," the teenager says admiringly. "She's going to do really good in school. Not like me."

Rachel makes the bed, while daughter Payten clowns for the camera.

It's a pleasant scene between a preschooler and an 18-year-old. The bedroom they are playing in is a cheerful place, decorated in girly pinks and yellows, a pile of stuffed animals heaped in one corner. With its two single beds pushed against the walls, it looks like a room where sisters might live, giggling and whispering secrets at night. And in fact the two girls do share the room. But they are not sisters; they are mother and daughter. Three-year-old Payten has the smaller of the two beds; her mother, Rachel Griffith, sleeps in the other. Rachel is 18. She had just turned 15 when her daughter was born.

"I always did bad in school," says Rachel, sitting on the floor of her mother's living room while Payten naps upstairs. "The kids I thought were cool didn't care about school, and I wanted to fit in with them. I just sat in class and talked with my friends. I got C's, D's, F's. I didn't care."

Growing up in a bad section of Northeast Philadelphia, Rachel's desire to "fit in" led her to hanging out with her neighbor boys, "playing fun games like Manhunt instead of doing girl things." At school, she was more likely to get into fist fights with other girls than make friends with them. "I was a tomboy, that's for sure. I didn't ever have girlfriends to speak of."

When she looked into the future, she saw only

vague, unrealistic pictures. "I wanted to be famous and rich, like everybody, I guess," she says with a shrug. "But I never really thought about how I would do that." Rather than make plans for her own life, she allowed other people to make decisions for her. "When I was in eighth grade, my mom said, 'You ought to become a dental hygienist.' I didn't really know what that was, but I said, 'Okay.'"

Education wasn't a high priority in Rachel's family. Her mother had graduated from high school, but her father had dropped out. No one was too concerned about Rachel's poor performance in school. But the atmosphere around the house was often tense for other reasons. "There was a lot of fighting. We kids were always getting in trouble, especially with my dad," Rachel explains. She has an older brother and sister, a twin brother, and another brother ten years younger than she. "My dad was the kind of person who seemed like the nicest guy in the world when you first met him. When I'd have friends over, he was always like, 'How are you doing? You want something to eat?' But if we kids did one little thing wrong, like not cleaning up after ourselves, he'd start beating us. He'd use his fists, a belt, a hanger, a cord, anything he could grab."

Rachel's parents eventually separated. Her mother now works two jobs to make ends meet, and the children still living at home pay rent to help out. Rachel's dad was making some efforts to re-connect with his family when he died unexpectedly in the fall of 2004. "Things had been getting better with him, actually," Rachel says sadly. "He was coming around a lot, making meals for us and so on. So it was hard to lose him like that."

As she was growing up, Rachel didn't feel much connection to any adult in her life. Her parents had a large family and their own problems to deal with, so, in her words, "We never really talked that much." At school, the only attention she got from teachers was related to her bad behavior. "They never said

Holding Payten's baby blanket, Rachel talks about her life today.

much to me except things like, 'You've got detention again.' I don't remember anybody ever talking to me about how I could do better in school or nothing like that."

Without any close girlfriends to talk to, she turned more and more to boys for friendship and attention. When Rachel was in seventh grade, she noticed Angel, a boy at her school. He was 15; she was 13. Angel was quiet and good-looking; "all the girls liked him." He lived in Rachel's neighborhood, and she and he began to walk home from school together. Sometimes they'd go to his house to hang out.

Eventually Angel asked her to have sex. Once again, Rachel let someone else make an important decision for her. "I didn't really know anything about sex," Rachel says. "I'd never talked with my parents about it, or learned anything about it at school. So when he asked me, I just said okay. It was like, if he asked me, I had to do it. That was pretty stupid."

The relationship was a secret one; there was absolutely no one she could tell. "He wasn't my boyfriend; we never were together at school. I would have been embarrassed to let anybody know about it."

Rachel knew that sex could lead to pregnancy,

but she thought that at 13 she was too young to worry about that. And Angel used protection.

While she was still occasionally sleeping with Angel, Rachel met her first boyfriend, Kenny. This relationship was out in the open; she and Kenny would even have sleepovers at each other's houses, with their parents' permission. "I guess they thought we were too young to be doing anything," Rachel says, with a disbelieving shake of her head.

As she entered ninth grade, Rachel was growing into a pretty young woman, and boys began paying more attention to her. She broke up with Kenny to date other boys. Because she was already sexually active, it was hard for her to think of reasons to say "no" to sleeping with other people. She was still having sex occasionally with Angel and Kenny when she met another boy, Travis. They had sex just one time.

Why was she sexually involved with so many partners, at such a young age? Rachel gives the simplest, and the saddest, explanation imaginable. "I just wanted them to like me," she says. "I thought if I let them do it, they'd like me better."

Just after the school year began, her 4-year-old brother found a gun in the vacant lot beside the family's home. Instantly, her mother decided it was time to leave their increasingly dangerous neighborhood. "She said, 'That's enough!' and put our house on the market," Rachel says. "The idea was that we'd find another house before it sold, but bang, somebody bought it right away. So we were more or less homeless." Scrambling for a solution, the family decided that Rachel and her sister would move in with their paternal grandmother, who lived in the other side of their twin house, and finish out the school year in Philadelphia. The rest of the family moved to suburban Bristol, Pennsylvania, to live with Mrs. Griffith's mother.

With her parents away, Rachel's life went on much as before. She paid little attention to school. She hung around with boys, occasionally sleeping with Angel or

Kenny. One day, she and Kenny impulsively broke into an acquaintance's house and took some money. They were arrested, fined, and put on probation. Getting arrested didn't faze Rachel much. "I was just such a loser," she says of this time in her life.

She did notice that she wasn't getting her menstrual periods, but her cycle had never been regular, so she didn't think too much about it. When she began to gain weight, she told herself she had just been eating too much of her grandmother's cooking. Friends began to ask, "Are you pregnant?" Far from telling them the truth, she would indignantly say, "No! I'm a virgin!"

"Nobody knew the truth about me," she says today. "I was so in denial about everything."

Eventually, she could not hide the truth any longer. On one of her weekend visits to her parents, her mother made her take a home pregnancy test. When it came out positive, her mother said, "You'll get an abortion." With her usual willingness to let other people make decisions for her, Rachel agreed.

"I just wanted to do whatever my parents wanted," she said. "I didn't know anything, and I just didn't want them to get mad at me. I was ashamed and embarrassed, and I just wanted the whole problem to go away."

When Rachel was examined by a doctor, however, she learned she was nearly six months pregnant. A simple abortion was not an option; if she had an abortion at this point, she would have to go through labor and give birth to a stillborn child. "So my dad said, give it up for adoption," Rachel says. But as the reality of her pregnancy sank in, Rachel realized that she had strong opinions about what was going to happen next. "I said no. If I was going to have this baby, I was going to keep it."

But Rachel's denial about her situation wasn't over yet. When her parents asked who had fathered the child, she said the first name that came into her mind—"Angel."

"They said, 'Are you sure?' and I said, 'Of course! He's the only one it could be.'"

Back at school, Travis and Kenny both soon noticed her pregnancy. Worried, they asked her who the father was. "I told them both, 'Don't worry; it's Angel's.'"

But it was Rachel who was very worried. She knew that after the baby was born, she'd be expected to file for child support, and that she would need to legally prove the baby's paternity. She was also concerned that if the baby didn't look like Angel, who was Puerto Rican, it would be obvious that she had lied. She tried to distract herself by taking good care of her health, now that she knew she was pregnant. "I ate really healthy, and I took my vitamins," she says. "I'd never been a drinker or smoker or druggie, so I didn't have to worry about that hurting the baby." At school, people were "pretty nice." "They'd say things like 'Move aside! Watch that stomach coming down the hall!'" she remembers.

Rachel watches Payten play in the bedroom they share.

"But most people weren't cruel. Maybe behind my back, but I didn't care about that."

When school ended in the spring, she moved to Bristol to live with her parents and grandparents. It was a lonely, isolated summer, but Rachel didn't mind. "It was good, in a way," she says. "Here I was living out in the 'burbs, and I didn't know anybody. I just stayed at home and thought about myself and the baby that was coming. I read books about pregnancy and bringing up children." Because she had babysat a good deal in the past, and helped care for her little brother, Rachel knew the basics of baby care—changing diapers, feeding, giving baths, and so on. "I knew that being a mother would be a lot more than that, but at least I knew that much." During the summer, Rachel also attended a "day camp" run for teen mothers by a local community organization. There counselors taught her about nutrition, discipline, child safety, child development, and other important issues. They also told her far more than she had known before about the different kinds of birth control and how to use them. In addition, the camp gave Rachel a chance to meet and talk with other young girls who were pregnant or had babies. For a girl who had never had many girlfriends, this was a valuable chance to make some friends.

Rachel went into labor on the morning of August 3. That evening at 7, she was still in a hospital room where a TV set was on. *The Simpsons* had just come on. Her labor was intensifying, and a nurse asked if she was ready to go to the delivery room. Rachel glanced at the cartoon show and said, "No, I want just another half-hour. It's my last thirty minutes to be a kid."

"I knew that, once I went into that delivery room, I'd be a mom forever," she says. "I knew everything would change."

Payten came into the world at a healthy 7 pounds, 12 ounces. Rachel plunged into caring for her daughter, showing a maturity that was surprising for a 15-year-old who had previously taken little responsibility for her life. "I did everything just like they'd taught me in the hospital," she remembers. "I got her on a great schedule, and I wrote down every feeding, every nap, every wet diaper. I read to her and talked to her and put her in her swing. Lots of moms don't read to their children until they're old enough to understand, but I did from the beginning. That's how they learn! And it worked, because Payten is so smart."

Rachel spent three weeks inseparable from the baby before starting school in the fall, this time at the county technical school, where she studied dental hygiene. "I hated leaving Payten, but I didn't want to be one of those teen moms who drop out of school." Academics were still a struggle for her, but now that she had a goal in mind, her grades gradually improved. She also took on a part-time job at McDonalds to pay for the baby's necessities. Her parents had made it clear that she, not they, would support Payten.

Although things were going well with her baby, Rachel still had a difficult obstacle to face: determining who the child's father was. Blonde, blue-eyed Payten did not look like Angel's daughter. Still, Rachel had been telling everyone he was responsible for so long that she had nearly convinced herself. But when Angel took a paternity test (done by using a cotton swab to gather sample cells from inside the mouth, then testing them), it showed that he could not have fathered Payten.

Rachel then had to make the difficult call to Kenny, and tell him he needed to submit to a paternity test. That test, too, was negative. "And so then I had to call Travis," she says. "That was pretty awful. I hadn't talked to him for so long, and the last thing I had told him was, 'Don't worry; it's not yours.' So here I was saying, 'Hey, you have to go for a test. I think she's yours.' He was very, very upset. But he went, and it turned out she was his daughter."

Since then, Travis has paid a small amount of monthly child support, and he visits Payten about once a week.

When Payten was a year old, Rachel's parents got their own house in Croydon, Pennsylvania, a town nearby Bristol. The family moved in, and, in Rachel's words, "things got rough."

"Mom and I fought all the time," Rachel says.

"Dad moved out. Mom kicked me and Payten out for about four months, and we stayed with a friend. She said I didn't help enough. But I clean the house, do the dishes, work as a dental assistant, go to school, and raise my baby. It hasn't been easy for me."

Rachel has returned to her mother's house, and she graduated from high school last spring. Her goal is to become as independent as she can, as quickly as she can, without neglecting her daughter.

"I'm working as a dental assistant, and I like it, but I want to go to college next year and study to become a hygienist, because they make more money," she explains. "I want to go part-time, locally, so I can be with my daughter, and I want to get an apartment for just the two of us. No roommates; I don't trust just anyone to be around her." She has applied for a subsidized apartment through the Housing Authority, but there's a long waiting list.

"If we get a Housing Authority place, that will just be a head start for us," she says. "I have a friend with

Still sleepy from a nap, Payten resists having her face washed.

a baby who's on welfare and really takes advantage.
She doesn't do nothing; she just sits at home all day.
I say to her, 'Why don't you get a job, or go to school

and learn to be independent? Isn't that what you want? What is your child going to think of you?'"

In the meantime, Rachel works, cares for her daughter, and plans for the future. From the moment she entered the hospital delivery room, she has accepted the idea that her normal teenage life is over.

"I don't go out and have fun partying," she says. "I see girls who are always out, acting like teenagers, leaving their children home with their moms, but I can't see doing that. This is my child, not my mom's. I decided to have her, so she's my responsibility. My mom won't even babysit, unless I'm working." As a result, people who want to be Rachel's friends have to understand the way her life is. "If someone doesn't want to hang out with a girl and her kid, then we don't hang out," she says, lifting her chin defiantly. "And if we do hang out, they need to respect my child. You don't smoke around her. You don't drink and act stupid around her. If you do, I'm outta there."

As far as dating goes, the same applies. "If I meet

a guy, I let him know up front: I have a daughter, and she comes first in my life."

Looking back at her early teen years, she tries to imagine what she'll tell Payten as she grows up. "I'll talk to her about sex, that's for sure. But not just sex; I'll talk with her about everything. I'll have a close relationship with her, so that she can tell me anything, ask me anything. I just will be the best mother I can possibly be to her."

Rachel figures Payten deserves that, and much more. "She has changed my life completely. If it wasn't for her, I would be a complete loser. I don't think I would have finished school, or gotten a good job. She kept me in school. She keeps me focused. I owe everything to her."

Johanna

Johanna Diaz

*J*ohanna Diaz got her first taste of what it meant to be a single mother the night after her daughter, Kiara, was born.

"Erik had taken me to the hospital and been with me during the delivery," she explains. Erik is Kiara's father. "Then he left, saying he was going to go celebrate, hand out lollipops and all that, and that he'd be back soon. But he didn't come. The whole day went by, and I kept thinking, 'He'll show up.'"

She finally fell asleep that night, then woke up at 3 in the morning. The couch where Erik was supposed to be sleeping was empty. "I lay there for hours," she says, "just watching the snow fall outside the window, my baby over in the nursery, and thinking, 'I'm alone.'"

Taking a break from housework, Johanna plays with her
Chihuahua, Blackie.

Johanna, now 22, is a Puerto Rican girl who
moved to Holyoke, Massachusetts with her family
when she was 7. Many of her relatives were already in
the area, and her cousins "helped" her learn English
by making fun of her efforts. "They'd laugh at me
when I tried to speak English," she says, laughing

herself at the memory. "They say, 'Nooooo, not like that—you sound so weird!!' "

Childhood in the Diaz home was happy and normal. Johanna's dad was a maintenance worker, and her mom stayed home with Johanna, her older brother and younger sister. "I got along okay with my dad, but I was super-attached to my mom," Johanna remembers. In fact, when Johanna was in fourth grade, she went through a stage during which she could not bear to be separated from her mother.

"Mom would walk me to school, which was just down the street from our house, and once we were there I'd have a fit. I'd cry and scream and refuse to stay." Her teachers and the school secretaries would try to bribe her with little gifts, but nothing worked. If her mother managed to slip away, Johanna would later ask to leave the classroom for a drink of water, then dash out the door and run back home. This went on for weeks, until her parents made her understand that if she refused to go to school, they might be taken to court and she could end up in a foster home. "Finally I settled down, and in fifth grade I got a Student of the Month award."

But Johanna's interest in school didn't last long. By the time she was in high school, she says, "I was in trouble all the time." She talked back to her teachers and spent her time in class chatting with other students. She did so poorly that she had to repeat ninth grade. Her parents scolded her and encouraged her to do better, but they spoke little English and were not deeply involved in her school life. And around the same time, Johanna had met her first boyfriend. She was 15; he was 17 and lived in the neighborhood. Soon after they began dating, they began having sex.

"We didn't use birth control," Johanna says, "and I didn't worry about getting pregnant. Why not? I can't even explain that to myself. We were so naïve, we didn't do anything to stop it. It was just being young, I guess. When you're that young and dumb, you just do what you're going to do without thinking about the consequences. You think you know it all, and that nothing bad can happen to you. Thanks to God I didn't get pregnant any earlier than I did."

Along with being "young and dumb," Johanna simply didn't know much about the facts of life. "Nobody every talked to me about sex," she remembers. "My mom did warn me about what would happen when I got my first period. She told me not to be scared, and if it happened at school, to tell a woman teacher and she'd help me. But that was all. Anything about birth control, or pregnancy, or diseases—nobody told me nothing about those."

Sometimes when a girl doesn't learn about sex at home, she has friends who fill in the gaps for her. This wasn't the case for Johanna.

"At school, I'd hear girls picking on each other. They'd talk about what they were doing, or they'd tease each other, you know, saying, 'You know you're not a virgin!' But I didn't want nobody to know. I didn't want word to spread about me. So if anybody said anything, I'd flat-out deny it. 'What are you talking about? Of course I'm a virgin.'"

And Johanna didn't have any close girlfriends to confide in. This is something she regrets today.

"I had girls I hung out with, but nobody really close. I didn't think I wanted that. I just wanted to have this little private world with my boyfriend, and nobody else knowing my business." She looks a little sad at the memory. "Now, I think it would have been good if I'd had a close girlfriend. She would have been someone I could have talked to and trusted. She could have given me feedback, helped motivate me. We could have said to each other, 'Hey, let's do good in school. Let's talk about what we want in the future.' Yeah, if I could go back, I'd do that differently. I'd want to have a best friend who could help me out."

As Johanna started tenth grade, she began noticing a new guy in the neighborhood. Erik was 20 and had just moved to Holyoke from Puerto Rico, where he had graduated from high school. To Johanna, he seemed like a big step up from the high school boys she knew. "He was handsome, one of the best-looking guys on the block," she said, ticking off his good qualities on her fingers. "He was attending college; he had a car; he had a job. He seemed so grown-up to me." Friends began passing messages back and forth between the two, and soon they were a couple.

Her relationship with Erik was not totally welcome news. "My mother, she is easily pleased," Johanna says. "Even if she didn't like Erik, she never would have said so. But with Dad, there was a bad vibe. He didn't say much, but I knew Dad didn't like him."

Being involved with Erik made Johanna even less interested in school. By the middle of her tenth-grade year, she told her mother she wanted to quit. Mrs. Diaz resisted, but Johanna's arguments finally wore her down. She signed the withdrawal papers. Johanna worked briefly at Burger King, then quit that too. After that, she says, "I did absolutely nothing. I just wanted to be lazy and hang out with my boyfriend."

But doing "absolutely nothing" got boring after a couple of months. "I got sick of myself," Johanna admits, and she began thinking maybe she should get her high school degree after all. She started attending a local GED program, and she found to her surprise that she enjoyed the classes.

Meanwhile, Erik had begun making extra money by selling drugs. Johanna didn't like that, but she ignored his activities as much as she could. She told herself that he was still a good guy. "Even though he was doing this bad thing, he was never aggressive, never abusive to me," she says. Then, just when she turned 18, Johanna realized her periods had stopped. A visit to the doctor told her what she had suspected: she was pregnant. Her "don't worry" attitude disappeared in a matter of seconds. "I sat there in the doctor's office and cried," she remembers. "Then I went home and told my mom, and she cried. 'How are you going to tell your father?' she kept asking."

Johanna cuddles Blackie while she talks about her life as a teen mom.

Indeed, telling her father was Johanna's greatest concern. "I told Erik, and he acted happy about it. But my dad was kind of strict and old-fashioned, and I was afraid to tell him. I kept it a secret from him for

51

another month. Finally, I wrote him a letter. I left it in the door, and went to Erik's for the night." The next morning, Johanna's dad telephoned her. To his daughter's amazement, he was crying. "He said, 'Come home, come home. Why didn't you tell me?' He said he wanted to see me and Erik both, and when we got to the house, he said, 'What's done is done. There's nothing to do now but accept what has happened.'"

Johanna remained at her parents' house, while Erik went back to his apartment. Johanna and her family preferred it that way, although not for the same reasons. "Dad had never liked Erik that much, so he didn't want to kick me out to go live with him," she explains. "And I didn't want to be at his place, either, because of the drugs. I didn't feel safe there, with people coming and going all the time, and never knowing if the cops would show up. I didn't want a life like that."

Although Erik had claimed to be happy about the

pregnancy, Johanna didn't see much of him during the next months. Staying at home, thinking about the new life she was about to bring into the world, she decided again to begin her interrupted GED studies. She learned about The Care Center, an organization in Holyoke that helps pregnant teens and teen mothers earn their high school degrees. Not only did The Care Center offer classes in ordinary school subjects, but it also offered activities: yoga, swimming, bowling, volleyball. Johanna became involved in the rowing team. She took child development classes, and participated in a problem-solving class called "Solutions." Care Center instructors coached the girls in filling out job applications, interviewing, and applying for college financial aid. At the Center, Johanna became close to other girls— the friends she wished she'd had earlier in life.

Kiara was born on December 18, 2000: a healthy, beautiful baby. But Erik's failure to visit Johanna in the hospital was a sign of things to come. After Johanna and her baby came home, Erik made himself scarce. Johanna took her three months' maternity leave from her studies at The Care Center and concentrated on caring for Kiara. Wanting to become more independent of her parents, she then applied for welfare and found a one-bedroom apartment of her own.

The day she moved into her new apartment, the phone rang. It was Erik, wanting to move in with her. "I was so stupid, I said yes," Johanna said. "I figured at least I had the upper hand—it was my apartment, and if things didn't go well I could tell him to leave. And I was still hoping he'd be a father to Kiara."

It soon became apparent, however, that Erik hadn't changed—except for the worse. Johanna began to suspect that along with selling drugs, he had begun using them. The guy whose good looks had originally attracted Johanna was becoming unkempt, ill-groomed. His hair was shaggy and greasy; he didn't shave regularly. Johanna found herself listening outside the bathroom door when Erik would lock himself in there; she heard him snorting something. She accused; he denied. They fought constantly. She kicked him out; she took him back. "It was crazy, letting him stay there," she says today. "I was in denial. I thought—I don't know what I thought. That it would be okay, somehow, even though I knew that was impossible." She returned to her studies at The Care Center, taking Kiara along every day to stay in the center's day care facility. While she was at the Center, she wondered what was going on at home. Would she find police in her house when she returned? Would a customer of Erik's become violent?

After three months of living this nightmare, fate stepped in. Erik was arrested for drug dealing and sentenced to two years in jail. Despite everything, his disappearance left a hole in Johanna's life. "I was sad he'd gone to jail. I had cared about him, and he'd been company for me for three years. I even had thought I loved him, but I was so young—who knows if I loved him or not."

But soon, Johanna began to realize how much of her energy—energy that she and Kiara needed—had been going into her dead-end relationship with Erik. "I looked at Kiara and realized how sad and stressed-out I'd been, instead of being able to concentrate on doing positive things for us," she says. "I started focusing—*really* focusing this time—on getting my GED and planning for college."

Johanna knew that she wasn't going to sail through the GED process. Her earlier lack of interest in school meant that she wasn't well-prepared. But even she did not know how difficult the process was going to be.

After months of preparation at The Care Center, she first took the GED test early in 2001. She failed. "I was disappointed, but I was okay," she says. "A lot of people I had taken it with failed, too, so I didn't feel like I was this big loser. We were all in the same boat." Not allowing herself to get discouraged, she studied for several more months and took the test

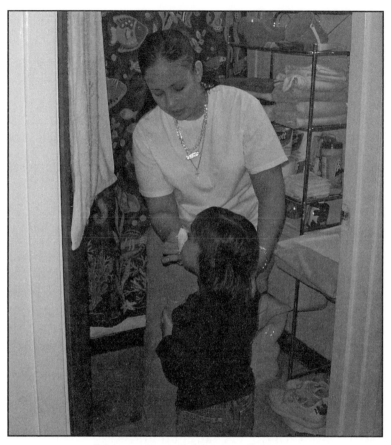

"Blow your nose!" Johanna tells Kiara.

again. Again, she failed. In December, she tried a third time. This test was especially critical, because GED test results in one calendar year are cumulative—that is, they are added together. Since she had passed some portions of the test earlier in 2001, she still had a chance to get her degree if she'd passed the other portions in December.

She failed again, by one point.

"That was heartbreaking," she admits. "I had to start all over again from scratch. Take the classes again, prepare to test again. I took the first 2002 test, and I failed again."

The next test was given in the summer of 2002.

"I thought I'd done well on it," she remembers. "In the weeks after I took the test, I checked the mail constantly. Finally a letter arrived. I saw the blue paper inside. I ripped it open and began screaming, 'I PASSED! I PASSED!!' " A man came out of a building and said, 'What's the matter??' I said, 'I passed my GED!!' He laughed and said, 'Well, congratulations!' And I ran upstairs and grabbed Kiara and danced around the apartment with her."

That fall, Johanna began classes at Holyoke Community College. She chose her major—Executive Office Technologies—took her placement tests, and was handed a schedule.

Although Johanna is usually a direct, confident person, she felt shy and lost in this new college environment. Instead of being assigned to "Business Math," a basic course she felt she needed, she had been placed in the more difficult "Accounting I" class. She was in over her head, and she panicked. "I *know* there was help available," she says today. "I could have asked for help there at the school, or there were people at The Care Center who could have helped me change my schedule or figure out what to do. Instead, when I saw I was failing accounting, I withdrew from school."

The next semester, Johanna had regained enough confidence to try again. She enrolled for four classes and did well in them all. But the next term, she hit another roadblock. Encouraged by her success the previous semester, she signed up for five classes. She was quickly overwhelmed. Once again, she withdrew from school.

Kiara and Johanna prepare scrambled eggs for lunch.

She got a job as a housekeeper at a local hotel. After five months, she concluded, "I hate this."

"The housekeepers get no respect; the pay is lousy; there's nothing you can advance to. And I realized, without more education, this is the only kind of work I'll be able to do."

Determined to keep working on her college degree, she made plans to return to Holyoke Community College at the start of the next semester. In the meantime, she left her housekeeping job and took a volunteer position as receptionist at Nueva Esperanza (New Hope), a non-profit social service organization in Holyoke. There, Johanna is finally doing work that she enjoys, where she feels respected, and where she is learning skills that will benefit her professionally.

Today, Johanna is looking forward to resuming her college studies. She has been dating Javier Vargas, a young jewelry salesman, for two years, and the two have recently become engaged. Kiara is four, and is a bright, talkative little girl who enjoys her friends at preschool.

Johanna is no longer in touch with Erik, but she

hears about him through the grapevine. He has been in jail again, and is in and out of drug rehab. "I don't expect him to ever ask for a role in Kiara's life. But if that happens, he'll have to go to court and ask for it that way," she says. "I've done a lot of work and there's been an awful lot of water under the bridge since Kiara was born. The life he leads is no life for my daughter."

Thinking ahead to Kiara's future, Johanna has some very firm ideas. "As Kiara grows up, I will be very open with her, and I will tell her all about my life," Johanna says. "I'll be involved in her school. I'll teach her about birth control, about sexually transmitted diseases, about taking responsibility for yourself. I won't say, like, 'Go ahead; have sex.' But I will tell her, 'Look, birth control is here for you if you make that decision.'

"Because, as much as I love my daughter, being a teen mom is really hard. When you're young, you think you know it all. You really don't. I want her to do better than I did. I'll tell her, 'Wait to become a mother. Go to college. Get a career. Don't let other people make your decisions for you. Wait until *you're* ready.'"

Rasheedah

Rasheedah Phillips

Rasheedah Phillips doesn't get a lot of sleep. She's up at 6:30 every weekday. On Mondays, Wednesdays, and Fridays she attends four classes at Temple University, where she is a senior. On Tuesday and Thursday she has two. She works as a research assistant for Temple's School of Social Administration, attends organizational meetings most weeknights, then hits the books far into the early-morning hours. She is keeping up this hectic schedule so she can finish her criminal-justice degree in three years, instead of the usual four.

The shadows around Rasheedah's eyes and the exhaustion in her voice make it clear that the schedule is taking a heavy toll on her. "I get pretty burned out," she admits. "I've thought about quitting

Rasheedah unloads the dishwasher as Iyonna plays with her magnetic letters.

school many times. But I'm here, and I'm going to stick it out."

Why Rasheedah is pushing herself so brutally can be told in one word: Iyonna. Iyonna is Rasheedah's

5-year-old daughter, born when Rasheedah was 14. "I keep going because I want something for myself," Rasheedah says. "But most of all, I want a stable life for Iyonna."

A stable life is something that Rasheedah herself doesn't know much about. She was born in Trenton, New Jersey, to a mother who was herself only 14. Rasheedah and her mother shared a house with Rasheedah's grandparents and an aunt, all of whom had become parents in their early teens. Other relatives and their children moved in and out occasionally. When Rasheedah was 3, her mother got married, and a few years later Rasheedah's half-brother was born. The family moved into their own apartment in Princeton, New Jersey.

Rasheedah assumed her stepfather was her real dad until one day when she was 7 and a stranger came to the door.

"I didn't know what was going on, but my grandma said it was okay for me to go with him," she remembers. "He took me to spend the day with his family, and people began telling me that this was my father." Rasheedah learned that he was in the service and lived in Japan, where he had a wife and three children. Since that first meeting, he has dropped in to visit Rasheedah every few years. "I feel nothing for him," she say, her voice both sad and bitter. "What bothers me most is why he waited so long to have any contact with me. I couldn't just throw a switch and suddenly feel like this stranger was my dad."

Within the next year, Rasheedah's mother and her husband divorced. Rasheedah was not sorry to see her stepfather go. "Mom was working two jobs and hardly ever around, and when she was gone he cheated on her, so when she was home they just fought." She and her mom and little brother moved back to her grandmother's house, but by this time her grandparents had divorced and both moved away. In the house were a young aunt and uncle, as well as the usual assortment of "down and out" relatives who came and went. Still, Rasheedah remembers this brief period as "the best time." "We moved into my mom's old bedroom, and for a little while I had her to myself. I got a little attention from her then."

Rasheedah finished her third-grade year in Princeton, then transferred to an elementary school back in Trenton. Soon after that, her mom met a new boyfriend, Troy.

"That's when things really started to go bad," Rasheedah recalls. "Troy moved in with us, and my mom began spending any spare time she had with him. He wanted to discipline me, act the father, but that was just ridiculous. He was even younger than Mom, barely out of his teens, and immature on top of that." Her mother became pregnant again and had yet another baby boy. Then an aunt and her two children moved into the house.

"It was just . . . lonely, more than anything else," Rasheedah says. "I had a roof over my head and food to eat, but emotionally—nothing. Now I understand a little better what was going on. My mother was really young, just a kid herself, and when she wasn't working, she wanted to be out having a good time. But I was deeply depressed. When I was 7, 8, 9 years old, I remember wishing I could die."

To make things worse, starting at a new school was always very tough on Rasheedah. And it was something she got a lot of practice in: with all her mother's moving around, she attended three elementary schools and two middle schools. Going into fourth grade, Rasheedah had several strikes against her. Most other students had already formed their friendships and cliques, and few people reached out to shy, depressed Rasheedah. Secondly, she was an unusually bright girl, a straight-A student, who'd attended a more advanced school in Princeton. In her new school in Trenton, she says, she got in trouble for knowing too much. "I could write in cursive; I could read better than the other kids. People resented me." And third, she had developed severe

Rasheedah helps Iyonna with a computer program.

acne, which made her the target of cruel teasing. Rasheedah remembers that time bitterly. "That's another way my mom just wasn't there for me. I was only in fourth grade, and I had serious acne. I need-ed to see a doctor, but she didn't do anything to help me." It wasn't until years later, when Rasheedah was old enough to seek medical care for herself, that she got the help she needed.

"There just wasn't any support at home," Rasheedah concludes sadly. "They didn't abuse me, but they didn't raise me, either. I raised myself."

What happened next was sad and shocking, but not surprising. Feeling unloved and unattractive, desperately wanting affection from someone, she began focusing on boys. She was spending a lot of time at the house of a friend named Mia. Mia had older brothers, and those brothers' friends hung around the house. Rasheedah noticed one 13-year-old boy she thought was cute. Her thoughts about him were the same ones any 11-year-old girl might have: "I wanted him to be my boyfriend. I began dreaming about my first kiss." The message that Rasheedah liked him reached the boy. He sent back a message of his own: that he was only interested in girls who would have sex.

"So I let him do it," says Rasheedah. "It was a horrible experience. I knew nothing. I honestly thought you had sex through your belly button. It was awful, and then it was over, and he never talked to me again."

Although losing her virginity had been a painful and humiliating experience, a few months later Rasheedah found herself in a similar situation at Mia's house. This time the guy was 19. And this time Rasheedah's mother somehow learned what had happened and came to Mia's house. When they found out that Rasheedah's mother was on her way, Rasheedah, Mia, and a few other kids ran away and wandered the city streets for a day and a half. "It was so cold, and none of us had any money," she recalls. "We ended up in some abandoned house, and then the cops found us and took us home."

At home, Rasheedah's grandmother slapped her,

and her mom was angry. She took Rasheedah to a gynecologist, then cut her off from using the phone and computer. "But still, we never talked," Rasheedah says. "There was no heart-to-heart, no discussion about why I was doing this." Instead, her mom enrolled her in boot camp at New Jersey's Fort Dix. For one weekend a month, the teenagers there lived in barracks, drilled, and learned about the military. "Mom thought it would teach me discipline," Rasheedah explains. "And I sort of liked it, but eventually I got into a fight with a girl who was talking trash, and they kicked me out."

Rasheedah shakes her head sadly. "The thing is— I was never a bad child. I really wasn't. I was making straight A's in school through all of this. But I was severely depressed. And all I really wanted was my mom's attention."

Soon after that, the family lost their house. Rasheedah's mother moved in with Troy's family, while Rasheedah returned to the house where her young aunt and uncle and their children were living. Now what little supervision Rasheedah once had was gone. Her behavior spiraled downward. Going into junior high school, she began to cut school frequently, drink and smoke, and experiment with drugs. Fights with other girls led to her being suspended over and over. Having sex with boys she barely knew became routine. The guys she slept with used condoms "occasionally," but for the most part, there was no effort to prevent pregnancy.

"I didn't let myself think about pregnancy much," Rasheedah says. "Even though I was sexually active, I didn't know much about birth control. It wasn't something I could ask my mom about. We were so disconnected from each other, I couldn't talk to her about anything so personal. And I guess some part of me wanted to get pregnant. To get Mom's attention. And to have someone of my own to love."

Rasheedah began to think more about pregnancy

when she was in eighth grade and a close friend had a child. From Rasheedah's point of view, it didn't look like a bad experience. "I saw how everybody catered to her, especially her mother," she says. "Her mom was always taking her to the doctor and stuff." When the baby was born, Rasheedah's friend gave it up for adoption.

At the end of her eighth grade year, Rasheedah's mom and Troy moved once again, into a townhouse in north Philadelphia. Rasheedah moved back in with them. Almost immediately, she connected with Brennan, a boy who lived in the same complex, and the two had sex. As a result of that one-time encounter, Rasheedah became pregnant, although she didn't realize it. "My periods were never regular—they still aren't," she says, "so I didn't have any idea I was pregnant for a few months."

Ironically, just a few weeks later, Rasheedah met a young man who wanted to be a real boyfriend to her, not just a one-night stand. She had gone to Great

Adventure theme park with some girlfriends, and there she met Gregg, who was 16 to her 14. "He was different than any guy I'd ever met," she recalls. "He was kind and loving and caring, and he soon became the whole world to me." The two began spending all the time they could together."

Rasheedah's mother noticed her daughter's changing body. "She kept asking, 'Are you pregnant?' and I kept saying, 'No, I'm just growing.' But around the beginning of school, in September, she dragged me to the doctor for a blood test. When it came back positive, she kicked me out for a few days. She was crying, disappointed. She kept saying, 'I'm so upset, I just can't stand to be around you right now.'" The reaction Rasheedah got from her grandmother was still more painful yet; the older woman cursed at her and called her names.

For Rasheedah, the most difficult task was telling Gregg that she was pregnant with someone else's baby. "I led him along for a while, letting him think it was his," she admits. "I *wanted* it to be his. But I knew the truth, and eventually I had to tell him. It was the most hurtful thing I've ever done. He cried for days. But he never turned his back on me."

Gregg encouraged her to get an abortion, but made it clear he would support any decision she made. Rasheedah considered the option, then rejected it. "I was already at least three months along," she says, "and while I'm definitely pro-choice, I didn't feel I could deal with an abortion." She wanted to give the baby up for adoption, but her mother discouraged her. "She'd seen kids who'd been in foster care forever because they hadn't found adoptive homes. She didn't want that to happen."

Rasheedah had to tell one more person about her pregnancy: Brennan. "The problem was, I didn't *know* Brennan," she says. The two had had almost nothing to do with each other since their sexual encounter. She was reluctant to approach him with such serious news. Finally, her mother told Brennan's mother, and soon after that Brennan knocked on Rasheedah's door.

"He said, 'So you're pregnant,'" Rasheedah says. "I said, 'Yeah.' He didn't really say anything. So I asked, 'What do you want me to do? Get an abortion?' And he said, 'Yeah.' That was pretty much the end of our conversation."

Rasheedah didn't want to have anything more to do with Brennan, but the new high school she began attending in September was also the one he went to. For a self-conscious young girl, this was a special kind of nightmare. "Brennan told his friends about me. Everyone stared at me; everyone gossiped about me, the pregnant 14-year-old. Teachers hated me, because I was this loose girl. There was no understanding. The only thing that saved me was the school's program for teen moms. There were caseworkers who talked to us about things like nutrition, and a place we could go to eat our lunch. It was a little escape from all the staring."

To make things worse, Rasheedah's pregnancy wasn't going well. In November, after she had experienced some premature labor, she was hospitalized. "I wasn't even allowed up to use the bathroom. I had to have a catheter and a bedpan." Lying in her hospital bed through Christmas and beyond, Rasheedah fell behind in her schoolwork and became severely depressed. Gregg could rarely visit; his father discouraged his relationship with Rasheedah, warning that she was just using Gregg to get a "step-in father" for her child.

Finally on January 20, Iyonna was born, two and a half months before her due date. She weighed four pounds five ounces—not too bad for a premature baby, but she still had to stay in the hospital, in an incubator, for three weeks. Rasheedah went home without her, miserable. "I felt like I'd failed her already."

"Baby blues" can happen to anyone. Many new mothers feel depressed and overwhelmed soon after

Iyonna gets a lift from her mom.

their babies are born. Usually, the blues go away after just a few days. But there is a more serious kind of problem called post-partum (meaning "after child-birth") depression. And post-partum depression hit

Rasheedah hard, sending her into a black hole of despair. Today, she struggles for words to express the misery she experienced as she faced the fact that she was now a mother. "I felt like my life was ruined," she says. "I didn't know how to do anything with a baby—I didn't even want to touch her. My mom took care of her at night, but when I was home with her during the day, all I did was sit and cry." She watched helplessly as her mother cared for the baby, showing a nurturing side that Rasheedah had rarely experienced herself. She felt torn by multiple emotions—jealousy of her mother's attention to the baby, fear that she would never be able to be a loving mother herself, deep depression at her situation, and confusion over the direction her life had taken.

During her moments alone, Rasheedah would sit on her bed and think about how she had once planned to go to college. "But after this happened," she says, "I looked at my mom's life and said to myself, 'That's what my life will be. I'll have more kids and I'll work multiple jobs just trying to make ends meet. *I'll never get anywhere at all.'*

In the meantime, Gregg was the one bright spot in Rasheedah's life. He came to see her whenever he could, tried to cheer Rasheedah up, and played with Iyonna, whom he called his daughter.

Rasheedah returned to high school, but by then she was almost too depressed to function. Iyonna was being watched during the day by a family friend, and more often than not, Rasheedah would cut school and go home to sleep. A doctor had prescribed anti-depressants and sleeping pills for her. One evening while Gregg was playing with the baby, Rasheedah locked herself in the bathroom and swallowed all the pills.

When Gregg realized that Rasheedah was in trouble, he broke down the bathroom door and got her to a hospital, where she was treated for the overdose. But doctors there realized that she was so severely depressed that she needed extra help. She was sent to

Friends Hospital, a psychiatric hospital in Philadelphia.

"I was relieved to be somewhere where I could
get help, but I was also angry, mostly at myself,
because I knew I wasn't crazy," Rasheedah says. "The
thing that bothered me most about being in a mental
hospital was that I had no control. They took away
anything I could use to hurt myself—my belt, my
shoelaces. I couldn't use the telephone; I couldn't go
for a walk; I couldn't make any of my own decisions.
They gave me medicine and I went to therapy, but I
don't know if any of that helped. What *did* help was
looking around at the other people locked in there
with me and thinking, 'Compared to them, my problems are not that bad. I don't belong here.'"

When Gregg came to visit her, bringing Iyonna,
Rasheedah had another realization. Looking at the
tiny baby, the innocent focus of her unhappiness, she
found herself thinking, "'I DO love her. If I die, who
will take care of her? My mom wasn't there for me. I

can't do the same thing to my daughter.' That thought gave me inspiration." After being at the hospital for a week, she was discharged.

"After that, things got a lot better between Iyonna and me," Rasheedah says. "We got into a routine, and I began to learn how to love her and interact with her." Rasheedah went into tenth grade telling herself, "I can do better than this. And I AM going to go to college." Having fallen so far behind in her studies, she had a hard time catching up. But gradually she pulled her F grades up to C's, and then to B's and A's. Support was hard to come by. "I heard a lot of discouraging remarks from people, like, 'You're going to drop out; teen moms always do,' or 'You can't go to college; you need to take care of your baby,' but I just ignored them."

Meanwhile, things were going badly at home. Rasheedah's mom was accustomed to taking care of Iyonna, and she resisted Rasheedah's efforts to step into the mothering role. And Gregg went off to

Shippensburg University, leaving Rasheedah feeling excited for him, jealous, and abandoned, all at the same time. Troy and Rasheedah's mother broke up, and there were several more moves before the family settled in a house in Philadelphia. Soon, Rasheedah's mom had a new boyfriend and was pregnant again.

Rasheedah was furious. "How could she get pregnant now, when we were so poor, and so cramped, and I so badly needed help and resources to get into college?" She had to enroll at yet another new high school, and as a new girl with a baby at home, she felt more alone and friendless than ever. "But by now, I didn't let myself care if I was alone," she says. "I just looked at school as my job. I went to school, I studied, I worked at McDonald's, and I came home to care for my child. That was it." She threw herself into her schoolwork and college research, once again achieving straight A's and applying for every scholarship she learned about.

By the time Rasheedah had graduated, she had

won scholarships worth a total of $9,000, and she had been accepted to Temple University, West Chester University, Chestnut Hill College, and Shippensburg University. She chose Temple because it had a strong criminal justice program, which appealed to her as a field of study.

A question remained: where would she live while she was in college? Her mother wanted her to leave Iyonna behind when she went to school, but Rasheedah was determined to raise her own child. She called Temple again and again, asking if there wasn't some way she could bring her daughter to school with her, and finally she was admitted to a building intended for married graduate students. She and Iyonna moved into a one-bedroom apartment there, and she began college.

Being Rasheedah, she didn't go easy on herself. A high school counselor had once mentioned that his son completed college at Temple in two years. Rasheedah told herself, "That's what I'll do." She

Rasheedah relaxes for a rare moment while Iyonna finishes her lunch.

began taking a crushing load of six courses. When it became apparent that she couldn't pull together enough money to graduate in two years, she extended her deadline one year.

"At the very beginning, college was wonderful, because Iyonna and I finally had our own place," Rasheedah says, "But then the first year got really horrible. I was working at Dunkin' Donuts and

McDonalds as well as going to class. It was really hard to find day care for Iyonna that I could pay for. Finally I got a scholarship that covered day care. But I was having problems with Gregg, and I was getting up at 6:30 every day and taking six classes, and I had *no* idea how hard the classes would be. For me, high school was academically pretty easy, and I just was not prepared." Socially, life was very difficult. Rasheedah's neighbors were older, married graduate students, few of whom had children. She didn't have time or resources to socialize with the younger students in her classes, and having a baby set her apart from them. Gregg, her only close friend, was far away at his own college. In October, Rasheedah snapped under the pressure. While Iyonna was spending the night at her grandmother's house, Rasheedah took another overdose of pills.

"I was just being stupid, just desperate," she says now. "I didn't want to die. I called for help right away, and was taken to the campus hospital. I began seeing a counselor at Temple, and I realized, 'This is ridiculous. I need to move on. Iyonna needs me.'"

Since then, Rasheedah has tried to learn to go a little easier on herself. She and Gregg are "taking a break" from their relationship. Despite her love for him, Rasheedah says, "I've basically been in a marriage since I was 14. I don't know who I am without him. He and Iyonna and I still do things together, but we're not boyfriend and girlfriend. I hope I'll be with him someday again, but I'm trying just to focus on the present now."

In spite of working many hours, being a mom, and studying, Rasheedah is trying to get more involved in college life. As a way of meeting more of her peers, she has joined a couple of organizations for African-American women, and she often eats in the college cafeteria, bringing Iyonna along.

"It's still not a normal college life, of course," she says. "I can't go to college parties. I can't go visit someone in her room, unless I bring my child along.

Not everybody understands that. It's hard to find friends who want to work around you having a child. And what little free time I have, I want to spend with Iyonna. So yeah, it gets lonely."

Although Rasheedah always planned to apply to law school after graduation, she is having second thoughts about law as a career. "I've really enjoyed the community service work I've done," she says. "Recently, I've been doing some work with a teen-father intervention program through Temple's social work division. We recruit teen fathers to get into the program, then encourage them to stay involved in their child's life. That kind of work is really inspiring to me."

Even though the end of her college career is in sight, Rasheedah still finds the road to be a rocky one. "I've thought about dropping out so many times," she admits. "I've applied to the Police Academy and other training programs. Sometimes keeping on going with so little support is really depressing. But my good grades have motivated me. That and my determination to make a good life for Iyonna. I just keep telling myself, 'I'm here. I can't change the past. But I'm going to make the most of the future, for both of us.' "

A Special Offer

If you enjoyed this book, Townsend Press

has a special offer for you.

Turn the page to learn how to obtain five

entertaining, readable books

free of charge

except for shipping and handling.

Why Become a Regular Reader?

Many people believe that reading is the very heart of education. Here is what they say:

1. Reading provides language power. Research has shown beyond question that frequent reading improves vocabulary, spelling, grammar, writing style, and reading speed and comprehension. If you become a regular reader, all of these language and thinking abilities develop almost automatically!

2. Reading increases the chances for job success. In today's world more than ever, jobs involve processing information, with words being the tools of the trade. Studies have found that the better your command of words, the more success you are likely to experience. *Nothing gives you a command of words like regular reading.*

3. Reading creates human power. Reading enlarges the mind and the heart. It frees us from the narrow confines of our own experience. Knowing how other people view important matters helps us decide what we ourselves think and feel. Reading also helps us connect with others and realize our shared humanity. Someone once wrote, "We read in order to know that we are not alone." We become less isolated as we share the common experiences, emotions, and thoughts that make us human. We grow more sympathetic and kind because we realize that others are like us.

And for many people, reading is a source of real enjoyment, opening the door to a lifetime of pleasure and adventure. By taking the time to walk through that door, you too may find that one of the great experiences of life is the joy of reading for its own sake.

Regular reading can, in short, change your life. The more you read, the more you know. The more you know, the more you grow.

A Special Offer

To promote your reading growth, Townsend Press will send you the following five books, edited for today's readers, at no charge except for shipping and handling.

Reading Changed
My Life!

Letters My Mother
Never Read

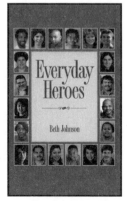

Someone to Love Me

Jane Eyre

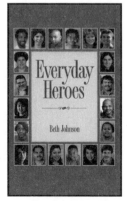

Everyday Heroes

Use the order form on the next page. Enclose five dollars to cover the cost of shipping and handling. You will receive these five highly readable books plus a free copy of a booklet entitled *60 Good Books to Read*.

A Special Offer

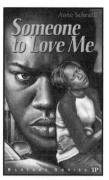

Letters My Mother
Never Read

Someone to Love Me

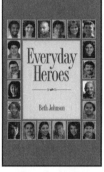

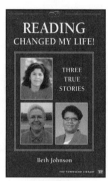

Jane Eyre

Everyday Heroes

Reading Changed
My Life!

*To learn more about these books and other books in the
Townsend Library, visit our website at **www.townsendpress.com***

Order Form

YES! Please send me copies of the five books shown.
Enclosed is five dollars to cover the shipping and handling.

Please PRINT very clearly. This will be your shipping label.

NAME

ADDRESS

CITY   STATE   ZIP

MAIL TO: TP Book Center
1038 Industrial Drive
West Berlin, NJ 08091